A Note to Parents

DK READERS is a compelling program for beginning readers, designed in conjunction with leading literacy experts, including Dr. Linda Gambrell, Director of the Eugenge T. Moore School of Education at Clemson University. Dr. Gambrell has served on the Board of Directors of the International Reading Association and as President of the National Reading Conference.

Beautiful illustrations and superb full-color photographs combine with engaging, easy-to-read stories to offer a fresh approach to each subject in the series. Each DK READER is guaranteed to capture a child's interest while developing his or her reading skills, general knowledge, and love of reading.

The five levels of DK READERS are aimed at different reading abilities, enabling you to choose the books that are exactly right for your child:

Pre-level 1 – Learning to read
Level 1   – Beginning to read
Level 2   – Beginning to read alone
Level 3   – Reading alone
Level 4   – Proficient readers

The "normal" age at which a child begins to read can be anywhere from three to eight years old, so these levels are only a general guideline.

No matter which level you select, you can be sure that you are helping your child learn to read, then read to learn!

LONDON, NEW YORK, MUNICH,
MELBOURNE, and DELHI

Series Editor Deborah Lock
Senior Art Editor Tory Gordon-Harris
Design Assistant Sadie Thomas
U.S. Editor Elizabeth Hester
Production Claire Pearson
DTP Designer Almudena Díaz

Reading Consultant
Linda Gambrell, Ph.D.

First American Edition, 2003
03 04 05 06 07 10 9 8 7 6 5 4 3 2 1
Published in the United States by DK Publishing, Inc.
375 Hudson Street, New York, New York 10014

Copyright © 2003 Dorling Kindersley Limited, London

Published in Great Britain by Dorling Kindersley Limited.

A catalog record for this book is available
from the Library of Congress

ISBN 0-7894-9991-6 (pbk. : alk. paper) -- ISBN 0-7894-9993-2

Color reproduction by Colourscan, Singapore
Printed and bound in China by L Rex Printing Co., Ltd.

The publisher would like to thank the following for their kind
permission to reproduce their photographs:
a=above; c=center; b=below; l=left; r=right t=top;

Ardea London Ltd: 23tr; **Corbis:** Wolfgang Kaehler 13c. Rob C.
Nunnington/Gallo Images 28tl; **Philip Dowell:** 26-27; **Getty Images:**
Arthur S.Aubry 30-31; Geoff du Feu 10tl; David McGlynn 4cl; Laurence
Monneret 31c; Tom Schierlitz 27br; Bob Stefko 18l; Kevin Summers
20-21; **Natural History Museum:** 2cra, 7cbr, 24bl, 24br, 25bl, 25bc,
25bcr, 32tl, 32bl; **N.H.P.A:** Stephen Dalton 15tr; David Middleton
4-5; **Oxford Scientific Film:** 8tl, 8-9, 9tc, Claude Steelman/SAL 6-7;
Jerry Young: 11bc, 26bl; **Getty Images:** Front cover: Steve Satushek

All other images © Dorling Kindersley
For further information see: www.dkimages.com

Discover more at
www.dk.com

READERS

LEARNING
pre-level
1
TO READ

Garden Friends

DK Publishing, Inc.

butterfly

garden

Meet the small animals in my garden.

snail

antenna

flower

butterflies

Hello, butterfly.
You are resting
on a flower.

wing

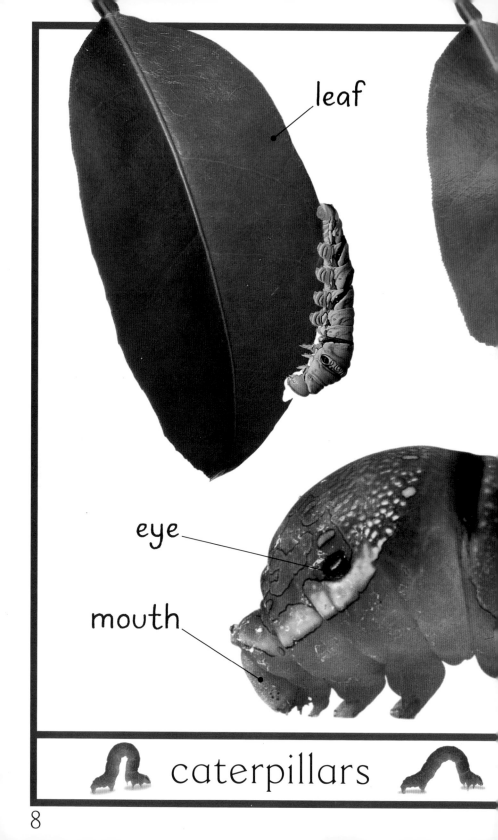

leaf

eye

mouth

caterpillars

Hello, caterpillar.
You are eating
a big leaf.

spot

ladybugs

Hello, ladybugs.
You have
many spots.

head

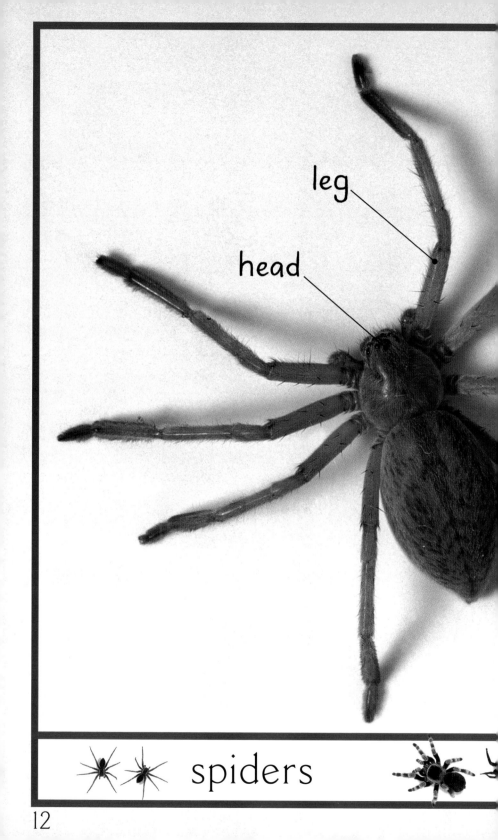

leg

head

spiders

Hello, spider.
You have spun
a big web.

web

flower

furry body

Hello, bumblebee.
You are drinking
from a flower.

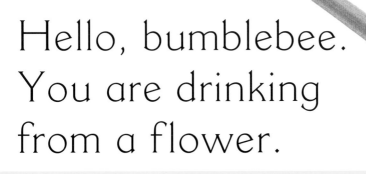

Hello, centipede.
You have many legs.

 centipedes

head

leg

Hello, dragonfly.
You are flying
around very fast.

dragonflies

wing

leg

19

baby snail

shell

snails

Hello, snail.
You have a baby
on your back.

soft body

worms

Hello, worms.
You are very long.

Hello, stag beetle.
You have very
sharp jaws.

wing

 beetles

ead

jaw

Hello, frogs.
You are hiding
in the grass.

foot

frogs

grasshoppers

wing

leg

Hello, grasshoppers.
Wow!
What a big jump!

dragonfly

What animals can

you find outside?

Picture word list

butterfly
page 6

caterpillar
page 8

ladybug
page 10

spider
page 12

bumblebee
page 14

centipede
page 16

dragonfly
page 18

snail
page 20

worm
page 22

beetle
page 24

frog
page 26

grasshopper
page 28